Formatting for File Conversion and Publication

HELEN WISNIEWSKI

ISBN10: 1-63199-429-8
ISBN13: 978-1-63199-429-6

Energion Publications
P. O. Box 841
Gonzalez, FL 32560

pubs@energion.com
energion.com

Foreword

For some years we at Energion Publications have struggled with the process of converting manuscripts from the author's format to the final, production ready layout. There are an amazing arrays of software solutions to help clean up text, but there's nothing quite like having it done right in the first place.

Many of the things in this booklet will be extremely familiar to those who regularly use word processing software, but writers often operate with the assumption that if it looks good on the screen, what you see is what you get.

That lasts until the first format change.

We commissioned this book to help writers use some basic, automatic formatting: Automatic footnotes, paragraph styles, and bibliographical formatting. We ask our authors to keep it simple. Choose a "Style" for your headings, use bold and italics, but above all, position *nothing* using the spacebar.

If you use the information in this booklet, you'll have little difficulty, and we'll be able to efficiently format your book for publication. We do hope these simple steps will be useful for others as well.

There are two sections, one for Microsoft Word and one for OpenOffice. The latter will generally be applicable to OpenOffice derivatives, such as LibreOffice.

Take time to learn how to use your tools. It will pay off in the end!

Henry Neufeld
Energion Publications

Formatting Using Microsoft Word®

Examples cover Word 2007, 2010, 2013, & 2016

Paragraph

Microsoft Word as opposed to a typewriter, was designed to remember formatting parameters; the author of the document just needs to write their thoughts, without the worry of having to "hit" enter each time the end of a line is reached. In the selection found below, you will notice in paragraph two, the author hit enter after each sentence, therefore, giving the appearance of a new paragraph each time. In the Home ribbon,[1] a resourceful author will select the Paragraph tool, to show or hide formatting marks, which ensures appropriate document format.

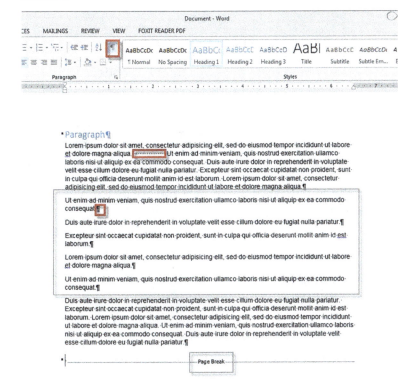

The following are symbols and what each represent:

Paragraph: ¶

Spaces: ·················

Page break: ·|————————————— Page Break —————————————

---

1   The term Ribbon, in Word, describes a two-dimensional set of controls, formerly known as the toolbar.

Styles

Styles are placed to create paragraph headings and in conjunction with the navigation pane, it is simpler to navigate within the document. Using heading styles to format your document gives your document a more organized and consistent appearance.

1. Highlight the text you want to use as a heading.

2. In the Home ribbon, view Styles and as you hover each style you are able to see how the text will appear, within the document. Upon finding the style you like, just click on it.

3. Utilize the navigation pane by navigating to the View ribbon.

4. Select the Navigation Pane checkbox.

5. The Navigation Pane gives the author the ability to "navigate" through the document very quickly without scrolling; clicking on a heading or page will take you to the desired section of the document.

Footnotes and Endnotes

The author places Footnotes and endnotes in documents to explain, comment on, or provide references to something mentioned in a document. Typically, footnotes appear at the bottom of the page and endnotes come at the end of the document or section, but can be changed based on author prerogative.

Add a footnote

1. Click where you want to add the footnote.

2. Navigate to the References ribbon.

3. Click Insert Footnote

TIP: You can also press Ctrl+Alt+F to insert a footnote.

4. Type the footnote text.

Add an endnote

1. Click where you want to add the endnote.

2. Navigate to the References ribbon.

3. Click Insert Endnote.

4. Type the endnote text.

Customize footnotes and endnotes

After you add your footnotes and endnotes, you can change the way they appear. For example, you can change the number format or the location in which they appear in your document.

1. Navigate to the Reference ribbon.

2. Click the Footnotes dialog box launcher.

3. In the Footnote and Endnote dialog box, select the options you desire:

    a. Under Location, choose Footnotes or Endnotes, and choose where you want it to appear.

    b. Under Format, choose a Number format, set the number you want to Start at, and then choose if Numbering is to be Continuous, Restart each section, or Restart each page.

4. Choose where you want to apply the changes, the whole document or the section you are in, and then click Insert.

Convert all footnotes and endnotes

The author has the ability to convert footnotes to endnotes, or endnotes to footnotes.

1. Navigate to the Reference ribbon.

2. Click the Footnotes dialog box launcher.

3. Click Convert.

4. Choose a conversion option and click OK.

5. Click Insert.

Delete a footnote or an endnote

1. Navigate to the Reference ribbon.

2. Choose Next Footnote or the drop-down arrow.

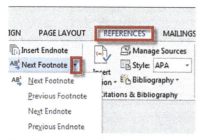

3. Select the footnote or endnote and then press Delete.

Bibliography Entries

Use Word to add and manage citations within your document. (Insert a citation, n.d.) By using the Reference tools, you can save time and eliminate common mistakes. These tools also save your sources, so you can quickly add more citations within your content. You can also add placeholders, if you prefer to insert citations after you complete your document.

Insert a citation from a new source

1. Navigate to the place in the document in which you would like to insert a citation.

2. Navigate to the References ribbon.

3. Click the drop-down for Insert Citation.

    a. Click Add new source.

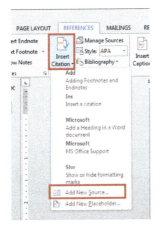

    b. Click the Type of Source drop-down to select the source.

    c. Fill-in the rest of the applicable fields.

4. In the Tag name field, give your document a unique identifier, using free text.

5. Click OK.

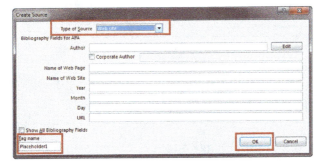

6. Select Style using drop-down menu.

7. Select Bibliography drop-down.

   a. Select either bibliography, references or work cited.

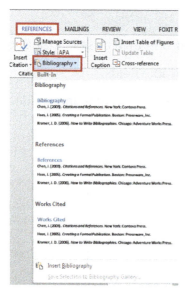

   b. Citations will automatically appear at the bottom of the document.

Add additional citations from a previously used source

1. Navigate to the place in the document in which you would like to insert a citation.

2. Navigate to the References ribbon.

3. Click the drop-down for Insert Citation.

4. Select the citation by Author or Tag name.

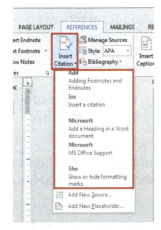

Bibliography

Adding Footnotes and Endnotes. (n.d.). Retrieved from https://support.office.com/en-us/article/Add-footnotes-and-endnotes-in-Word-61f3fb1a-4717-414c-9a8f-015a5f3ff4cb?ui=en-US&rs=en-US&ad=US

Insert a citation. (n.d.). Retrieved from https://support.office.com/en-US/article/Insert-a-citation-4003124f-c043-4ef7-8b7d-01604a778d8b

Microsoft. (n.d.). Retrieved from MS Office Support: https://support.office.com/en-US/article/Insert-a-citation-4003124f-c043-4ef7-8b7d-01604a778d8b

Microsoft. (n.d.). *Add a Heading in a Word document*. Retrieved from https://support.office.com/en-US/article/Add-a-heading-in-a-Word-document-9f632a5c-b33e-4b69-985b-7dcbbbb558ee?ui=en-US&rs=en-US&ad=US

Show or hide formatting marks. (n.d.). Retrieved from https://support.office.com/en-us/article/Show-or-hide-formatting-marks-c0460106-19d3-4441-986c-b655bffe6be4?ui=en-US&rs=en-US&ad=US

Formatting Using OpenOffice and Derivatives

Examples use OpenOffice 4.1.3

Paragraph

OpenOffice Writer as opposed to a typewriter, was designed to remember formatting parameters; the author of the document just needs to write their thoughts, without the worry of having to "hit" enter each time the end of a line is reached. In the selection found below, you will notice in paragraph two, the author hit enter after each sentence, therefore, giving the appearance of a new paragraph each time. In the tools ribbon, a resourceful author will select the Paragraph tool, to show or hide formatting marks, which ensures appropriate document format.

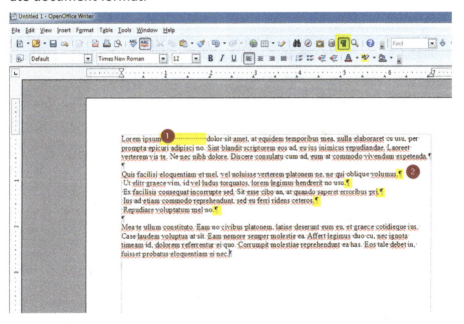

The following is the key for paragraph symbols used in OpenOffice Writer:

1. Paragraph: ¶

2. Spaces: ....

3. Page break: does not have a designation like Microsoft Word; it is a ¶ symbol

Styles and Formatting

Styles and Formatting used to create paragraph headings in conjunction with the Navigator, makes it simpler to navigate the document. Using heading styles to format your document gives the document a more organized and consistent appearance.

1. Place the cursor within the text of the area, which will become the heading.

2. Click on the drop-down for styles and formatting for a short list of formatting options or click on the styles icon and the full menu will be available.

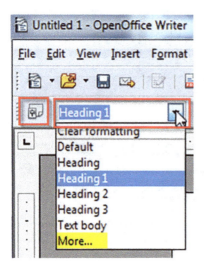

Once in the drop-down menu, if the choice is not available, select 'More...' and the full menu will appear as a pop-up menu.

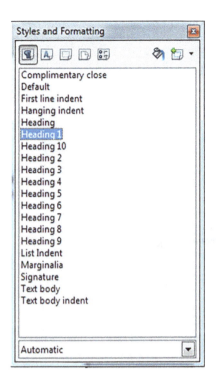

The author will also find styles and formatting icon on the right side of the document.

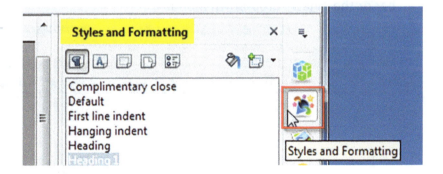

Otherwise, use the Format drop-down menu.

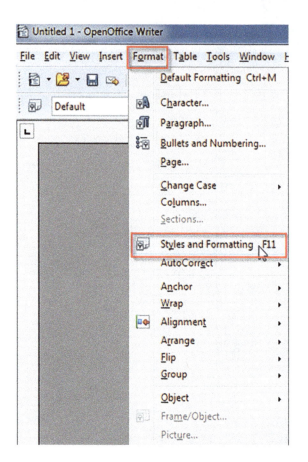

3. Utilize Navigator by either using the Navigator icon on the tool bar or the "View" drop-down menu.

18

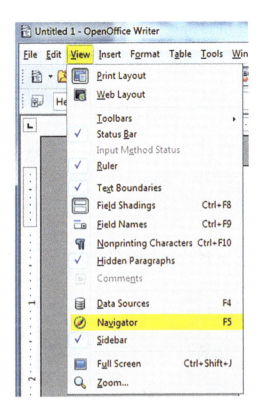

Alternatively, use the Navigator icon on the right border of the page.

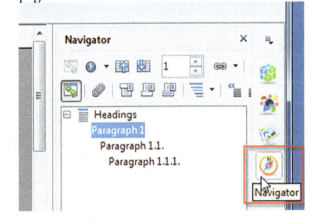

4. Depending how far you want to drill down into your headings, you will need to set up the Navigator. There will be a drop-down menu of heading levels, by selecting the "Heading Levels Shown" icon. The Navigator gives the author the ability to "navigate" through the document very quickly without scroll-

ing; double-clicking on a heading will take you to the desired section of the document.

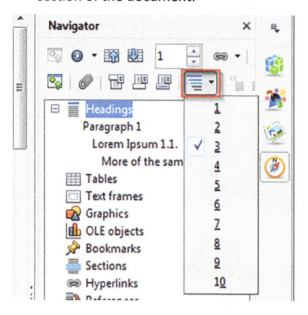

Footnotes and Endnotes

Footnotes and endnotes allows the author to explain, comment on, or provide references to something mentioned in a document. Typically, footnotes appear at the bottom of the page and endnotes come at the end of the document or section, but can be changed based on author prerogative.

Add a footnote or endnote

1. Click where you want to add the footnote.

2. Click on the 'Insert' drop-down menu on the toolbar.

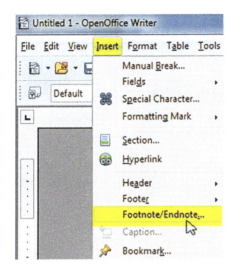

3. In the pop-up window, you will need to decide what type of numbering you will prefer; Automatic or Character. Also, choose type Footnote or Endnote. Click "OK" when finished.

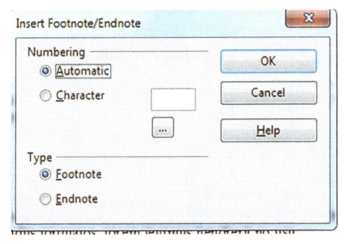

Bibliography

Finally, you can add and manage citations within your document, by using the indexing tools. These tools also save your sources, so you can quickly add more citations within your content.

Insert a citation from a new source

1. Navigate to the place in the document in which you would like to insert a citation.

2. Click the Insert drop-down menu.

3. Select Indexes and Tables and from the next menu select Bibliography Index.

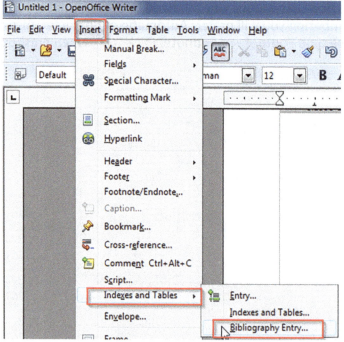

4. Fill-in 'Insert Bibliography Entry' form, to choose an existing citation, select 'From bibliography database' then click 'Insert.'

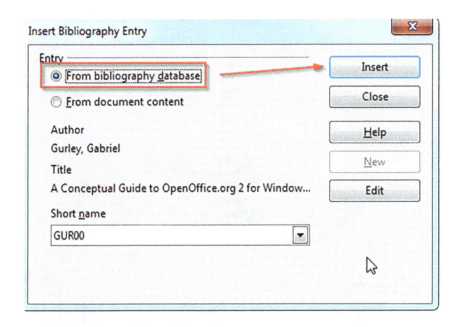

5. Create a citation by selecting 'From document content' then click 'New.'

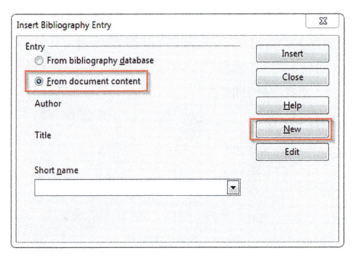

6. Fill-in the pop-up 'Define Bibliography Entry' form. The fields 'Short name' and 'Type' are the only required fields for this form.

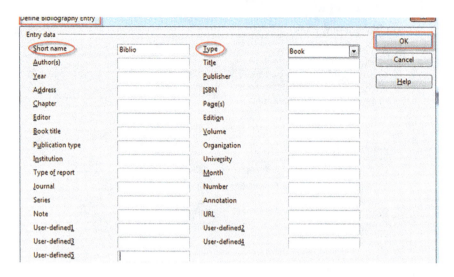

7. Click OK.

8. Click Insert only once or the citation will appear as many times as is selected.

9. Click Close to close the 'Insert Bibliography Entry' pop-up form.

www.ingramcontent.com/pod-product-compliance
Lightning Source LLC
Chambersburg PA
CBHW071554080326
40690CB00056B/2041